MW00890725

This Notebook
belongs to:

____

____

Made in the USA
Monee, IL
08 January 2022

88459262R00063